ABRAHAM

written by

Susan L. Lingo

Melissa C. Downey

illustrated by

Roy Green

STANDARD PUBLISHING
Cincinnati, Ohio

Scripture quotations designated by (ICB) are from the *International Children's Bible, New Century Version*, copyright © 1983, 1986, 1988 by Word Publishing, Dallas, Texas 75039. Used by permission.

Scripture quotations designated by (NIV) are from the *Holy Bible: New International Version*, © 1973, 1978, 1984 by the International Bible Society. Used by permission of Zondervan Bible Publishers and the International Bible Society.

Library of Congress Catalog Card Number 91-067044

ISBN 0-87403-915-0

Copyright © 1992 Susan L. Lingo, Melissa C. Downey
Published by The STANDARD PUBLISHING Company, Cincinnati, Ohio.
Division of STANDEX INTERNATIONAL Corporation. Printed in U.S.A.

ABRAHAM

Abram couldn't believe what he had heard! What was it that God had promised? Oh there was so much! Yes! He remembered! God promised to make Abram a great nation and bless him. God promised that Abram's name would be great. God promised blessings for those Abram blessed and curses for those who cursed Abram. Wow! Abram's thoughts raced! God had promised him *so* much!

But God had also told Abram to do something. Now what was it that God wanted Abram to do? Abram could hear God's words in his heart, "Leave your country, your people and your father's household, and go to the land I will show you."

Abram did not hesitate. He began packing his many belongings. Abram loved God. He listened to God and obeyed Him. Abram was a very successful shepherd in Hebron when God told him to leave. Sarai, his wife, was known for her beauty. Together, they prepared for the journey. Lot, Abram's nephew went along, too. Together with their servants and flocks, they began the long journey to the land God had chosen.

Finally, when they had reached the great tree of Moreh at Shechem in the land of Canaan, God said to Abram, "To you and your descendants I will give all this land. Your descendents will be as many as the dust of the earth." Abram moved on to live near the great trees of Mamre at Hebron. There he built an altar to God.

Abram asked the Lord, "What can you give me since I have no child—no one to inherit my wealth?"

God took Abram outside and said, "Look up at the heavens and count the stars—if you can count them! So shall be your descendants."

Abram believed God. But still no child was born to Abram and Sarai. Years passed. When Abram was 99 years old, God said, "No longer will you be called Abram. Instead you will be called Abraham which means Father of Many Nations. And Sarai will no longer be called Sarai. Instead she will be called Sarah. I will bless her, and she will be the mother of many nations."

Abraham laughed, for he was too old to have a child. Again time passed and again the Lord came to Abram and repeated His promise. This time Sarah heard what the Lord said. She laughed when God said they would have a child. She was too old to have children.

The Lord asked, "Is there anything too hard for the Lord?" Abraham and Sarah continued to wait.

Just as God promised, Sarah became pregnant and had a son. Sarah

©1992 Susan L. Lingo, Melissa C. Downey
Permission is granted to reproduce this page for classroom use only—not for resale.

was 90; Abraham was 100. Abraham named the son Isaac, which means laughter, for he and Sarah had laughed to think they could have a son at their old age.

Sarah said, "God has brought me laughter and everyone who hears about this will laugh with me" (Genesis 21:6). Abraham had walked with God many years. Abraham obeyed God, for Abraham had learned that God's way is always best. In all things Abraham trusted God. God wanted Abraham to realize how much he truly loved God. This would help Abraham grow closer to God. It would help Abraham to become more like God in his heart.

So God asked Abraham to be willing to sacrifice his one and only son Isaac. God said, "Take your son, your only son Isaac whom you love, and go to the land of Moriah. On a mountain there you shall give him up as a burnt offering to me."

Abraham obeyed God. The next morning, he saddled his donkey and took with him two servants and Isaac. After three days, Abraham arrived at the mountain God had chosen. Leaving the two servants at the bottom of the mountain, he and Isaac began to climb.

Isaac carried the wood for the offering. Turning to his father as they climbed, Isaac said, "The wood and fire are here for the offering, but where is the lamb?" Abraham replied, "God will provide a lamb."

When they reached the place God had told him about, Abraham built an altar and arranged the wood on it. Then he bound Isaac and placed him on the altar. When he reached out to take his knife to slay his son, the angel of the Lord said, "Abraham! Abraham! Do not lay a hand on the boy. Do not do anything to him. Now I know that you fear God because you have not withheld from me your son, your only son."

Abraham looked up and there was a ram, tangled by his horns in the bushes. Abraham offered the ram as a burnt offering to God.

Abraham trusted God. He had so much faith that he was willing to give his precious son to God. The Bible tells us that God loved us so much that He sent His Son Jesus to earth to teach us about God and to die on the cross to pay the price for our sins.

John 3:16 says that "God so loved the world [us] that he gave his one and only son, that whoever believes in him shall not perish but have eternal life."

Abraham and Sarah

In long-ago days, there lived a man named 🧔. 🧔 was a good man and had given his ♡ to God. 🧔 spent his days tending flocks of 🐑 and loving his wife 👩.

1 day, the Lord asked 🧔 to leave his 🏠. God said He would lead 🧔 to the Promised Land. God promised 🧔 that he would be the father of many 👨‍👩‍👧; that 🧔 would have more 👨‍👩‍👧 than ⭐ in the sky!

So 🧔, 👩 and Abraham's nephew Lot packed up their ⛺ and their 🐑 and followed the Lord.

🧔 and 👩 had no 👶, and this made them feel 😢. God made another promise to 🧔 and told him that he and 👩 would have a 👶. 🧔 and 👩 were **2** old to have a 👶, so 👩 just 😂.

But God always keeps His promises! Soon 🧔 and 👩 had a beautiful 👶 boy! 👩 said, "God has brought me laughter, and everyone who hears about this will laugh with me" (Genesis 21:6). And because God had given 🧔 and 👩 such joy, they named the 👶 Isaac, which means laughter!

©1992 Susan L. Lingo, Melissa C. Downey
Permission is granted to reproduce this page for classroom use only—not for resale.

Abraham's World

Ur in Chaldea was Abraham's hometown. Villas, houses with 12 to 14 rooms, lined the streets of Abraham's neighborhood. Each villa had indoor plumbing—very unusual that long ago (3900 years ago). Ur was the most advanced city in the world.

God told Abraham's family to leave Ur and to travel to Haran. From Haran, they traveled with their families and herds to Hebron. After staying there, they made a journey to Egypt and then returned to Hebron. All this traveling was pretty amazing as they traveled on foot and by donkey.

Using the map below, can you figure out how many miles Abraham traveled? Each foot (　　) = 75 miles.

1. How far is it from Ur to Haran? _____ feet x 75 = _____ miles
2. How far is it from Haran to Hebron? _____ feet x 75 = _____ miles
3. How far is it from Hebron to Egypt? _____ feet x 75 = _____ miles
4. How far is it from Egypt back to Hebron? _____ feet x 75 = _____ miles
5. Add the miles together. How many miles did Abraham travel? _____ miles

(Answers: 1. 8, 600; 2. 8, 600; 3. 4, 300; 4. 4, 300; 5. 1,800)

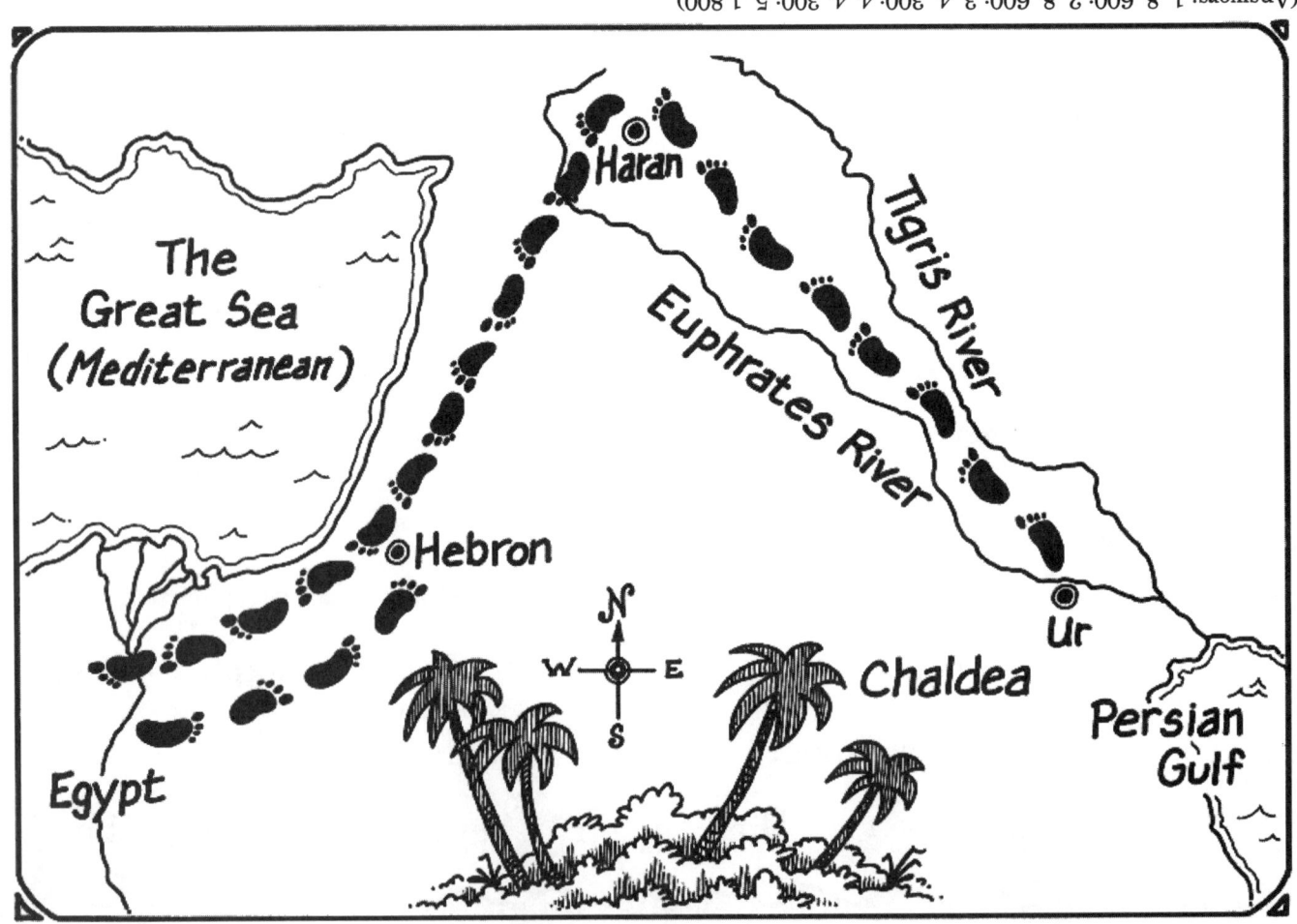

©1992 Susan L. Lingo, Melissa C. Downey
Permission is granted to reproduce this page for classroom use only—not for resale.

Faithful Follower

MEMORY WORK

"It was by faith Abraham obeyed God's call to go to another place that God promised to give him. He left his own country, not knowing where he was to go."

Hebrews 11:8 (ICB)

Blindfolded Following

How do you think Abraham felt being led, not knowing where he was going? Certainly he needed to listen very carefully! If you were in Abraham's place, how hard do you think you would have to listen?

Try this!
You will need a blindfold and a large area with obstacles.

This activity may be done in or out of doors. The object is for the adult leader to guide the blindfolded student through an area in which there are three to four obstacles (going around chairs, under a table, in and out of a large box, etc.). No more than three to four obstacles should be used. The leader should read the following instructions to the students.

1. The student is to pretend to be Abraham.
2. He is to listen carefully to the leader's directions in order to know where to go.
3. He must trust the leader to give him the best directions possible to be successful in completing the journey.

(Clear, precise directions must be given to guide the student successfully through the area. Students should not see the area before the activity. After all students have completed the course, discuss the experience.)

1. How did you feel when you didn't know where you were going?
2. Do you think Abraham felt that way?
3. How hard did you have to listen? What happened when you didn't listen well?
4. What did you need to do in addition to listening? (trust the leader)
5. When you went through the activity you could hear the sound of your leader's voice with your ears. How do we hear the directions God gives us? (with our hearts)

To close the activity, read the memory verse again.

©1992 Susan L. Lingo, Melissa C. Downey
Permission is granted to reproduce this page for classroom use only—not for resale.

"Abram believed the Lord..." Genesis 15:6

Like Abram, to truly believe in the Lord means placing our faith in Him. Complete the following math problems to find out what happened when Abram believed in the Lord.

Check your answer in Genesis 15:6 (ICB).

$\overline{1\times0}$ $\overline{24\div2}$ $\overline{12\div2}$ $\overline{30+8}$ $\overline{24-10}$ $\overline{4\times2}$

$\overline{11\times2}$ $\overline{14\times2}$ $\overline{30+4}$ $\overline{12\div2}$

$\overline{2\times0}$ $\overline{3+1}$ $\overline{2\times2}$ $\overline{16\div2}$ $\overline{15\times2}$, $\overline{36\div2}$ $\overline{16-8}$ $\overline{36\div6}$

$\overline{2-2}$ $\overline{1+1}$ $\overline{2\times17}$ $\overline{4-4}$ $\overline{12\times2}$ $\overline{40-4}$

$\overline{5+5}$ $\overline{3\times0}$ $\overline{20-4}$ $\overline{28+10}$ $\overline{7\times2}$, $\overline{6-6}$ $\overline{13\times2}$ $\overline{2\times3}$

$\overline{2\times19}$ $\overline{28\div2}$ $\overline{1\times0}$ $\overline{35+3}$ $\overline{12-2}$ $\overline{0\times16}$ $\overline{4\times4}$ $\overline{34+4}$ $\overline{16-2}$

$\overline{18+6}$ $\overline{7-7}$ $\overline{12\div2}$ $\overline{5+3}$ $\overline{18-4}$ $\overline{12+4}$ $\overline{6\times4}$

$\overline{26+8}$ $\overline{13+3}$ $\overline{6+6}$ $\overline{17-3}$ $\overline{48-10}$ $\overline{22+22}$ $\overline{7+9}$ $\overline{24+14}$ $\overline{8+6}$

$\overline{15-3}$ $\overline{21+7}$ $\overline{2\times3}$

A=0 B=2 C=4 D=6 E=8 F=10 G=12 H=14 I=16 J=18
K=20 L=22 M=24 N=26 O=28 P=30 Q=32 R=34 S=36
T=38 U=40 V=42 W=44 X=46 Y=48 Z=50

©1992 Susan L. Lingo, Melissa C. Downey
Permission is granted to reproduce this page for classroom use only—not for resale.

Abraham was very special to God—so special that he was called God's friend! Work to memorize the following Scripture verse. Then make Abraham and see if you can lift his arms to give his Father-friend a big hug!

"Abraham was called God's friend" (James 2:23).

You need: 4 brads and a craft stick

Directions:
1. Color and cut out pieces.
2. Glue head to the body and attach arms and legs at dots with brads.
3. Staple Abraham to craft stick.

©1992 Susan L. Lingo, Melissa C. Downey
Permission is granted to reproduce this page for classroom use only—not for resale.

Abraham Gave a "Lot"

Selflessness is placing others' feelings, wants, and needs before our own. It is loving others enough to give them the very best of everything! Read Genesis 13:1-15 (NIV) and then complete the puzzle below to find out how selfless Abraham was.

1. Abraham became very wealthy in _ _ _ _ _ _ _ _ . (vs.2)
                                                                              13 1

2. Now Lot, who was with Abraham, also had _ _ _ _ _ . (vs. 5)
                                                                                   16

3. But the land could not _ _ _ _ _ _ _
                                 29
   them if they stayed _ _ _ _ _ _ _ _ . (vs. 6)
                              5

4. The herdsmen began to _ _ _ _ _ _ _ .
   (vs. 7)   22

5. Abraham said to Lot, "Let's not have any quarreling . . . for we are _ _ _ _ _ _ _ _ .
   (vs. 8)   7   18
   Is not the _ _ _ _ _ land before you?" (vs. 9)
                  10

6. So Lot chose the green plain of the
   _ _ _ _ _ _ (vs. 11), while Abraham stayed
   in _ _ _ _ _ _ (vs. 12)
      8

7. God saw how selfless Abraham had been, and He gave Abraham all the land he could see for his _ _ _ _ _ _ _ _ _ forever. (vs. 15)
     3 25

Now arrange the numbered letters in the correct spaces.

 God Smiles upon _ _ _ _ _ _ _ _ _ _ _ .
                                    16 7 22 3 10 5 1 18 8 13 25 29

©1992 Susan L. Lingo, Melissa C. Downey
Permission is granted to reproduce this page for classroom use only—not for resale.

Visitors' Visions

Abraham and Sarah heard about the forthcoming birth of their son Isaac in a wonderous way! Use your Bible (ICB) and read Genesis, chapter 18. Then fill in the missing words below to complete the story of the visit of the three mysterious men!

The Lord _____ (vs.1) to Abraham one hot afternoon. As Abraham looked up, he noticed _____ ____ (vs.2) standing nearby, and he ran to bow _____ (vs.2) before them. Abraham asked them to stay and eat before continuing their _____ (vs.5).

While the three visitors ate, they asked **A**braham, "Where is your _____?" (vs.9) He told them Sarah was in their tent. The _____ (vs.10) then **s**poke and said, "I will _____ (vs.10) return to you about this time a year from now. At that time _____ _____ _____ (vs.10) will have a _____." (vs.10)

Sarah, who was _____ (vs.10) from the tent, _____ (vs.12) at the thought of having a baby **n**ow that she was so old! The Lord said to Abraham, "Why did _____ (vs.13) laugh? . . . Is anythin**g** too _____ (vs.14) for the Lord? No!"

Sarah was _____ (vs.15) and lied to the Lord saying, "I didn't laugh." But th**e** Lord knew the truth!

Who were these three visitors? Unscramble the highlighted letters in the story to find out!

_____ of the Lord.

©1992 Susan L. Lingo, Melissa C. Downey
Permission is granted to reproduce this page for classroom use only—not for resale.

Sarah Flips for Isaac

Sarah, unhappy and childless, laughed when God promised her a son. But Sarah soon learned of two great joys: her son, Isaac; and the truth that nothing is too hard for the Lord!

Directions:

1. Color, cut, and glue pattern to stiff paper.
2. Tape a tissue to the - - - - - - - line for Sarah's skirt.
3. Make Sarah flip for her precious son, Isaac.

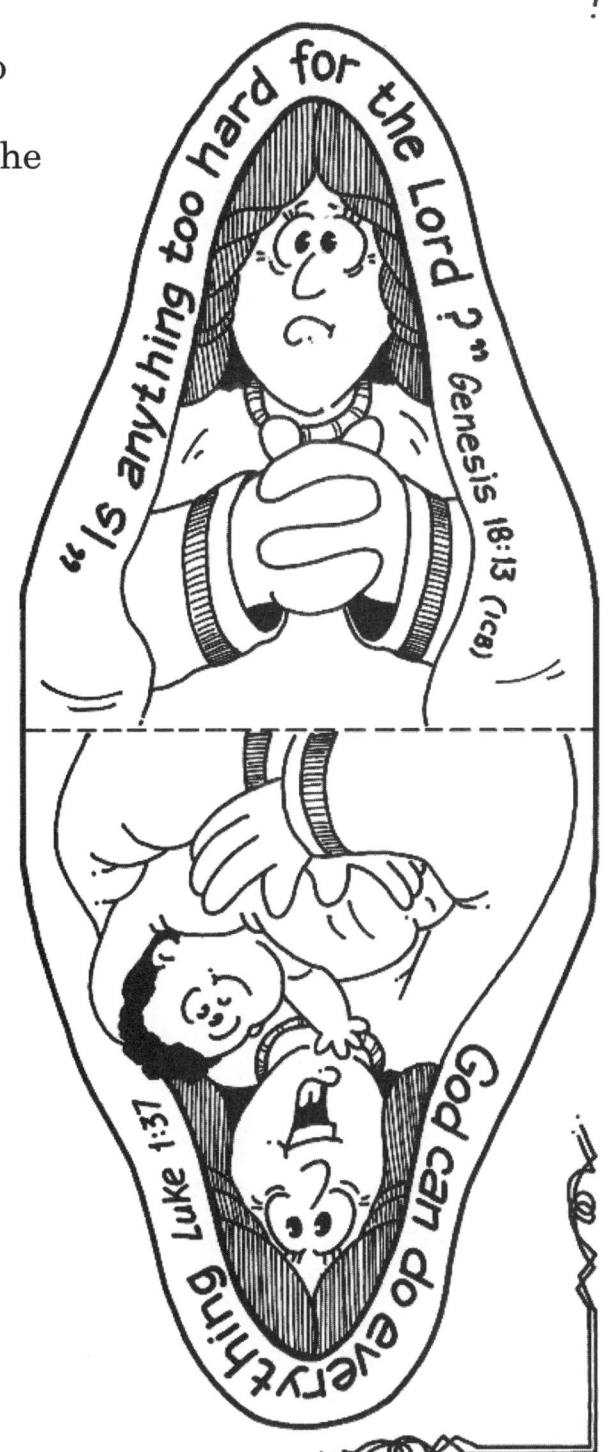

©1992 Susan L. Lingo, Melissa C. Downey
Permission is granted to reproduce this page for classroom use only—not for resale.

In the Bible we read that Abraham was called the "father of nations." But the Bible also tells us Abraham was called a name even more special. Use your NIV Bible and the book of Genesis to fill in the missing words in the lines below. Then use the numbered letters to fill in the blanks on the stone at the bottom of the page and discover Abraham's special name!

1. Abraham's son was called __ __ __ __ __ (21:3).
                8   24   9
2. Abraham had a wife named __ __ __ __ __ (17:15).
             10   5   26
3. The Lord did what He had __ __ __ __ __ __ __ __ (21:1).
                  3   2
4. Abraham would be a great __ __ __ __ __ __ (12:2).
             14   20
5. Abraham kept his sheep in a __ __ __ __ __ (21:28).
            1   12   7   16
6. Sarah said, "God has brought me __ __ __ __ __ __ __ __ (21:6).
                 4   15   13
7. Abraham built an altar to the __ __ __ __ (12:7).
             23   11   22
8. Sarah and Abraham lived in a __ __ __ __ (13:18).
                 19
9. Abraham was __ __ __ __ __ __ __ (14:19).
        18   25   17
10. Sarah was Abraham's __ __ __ __ (18:10).
                6   21

from James 2:23

©1992 Susan L. Lingo, Melissa C. Downey
Permission is granted to reproduce this page for classroom use only—not for resale.

Sheep and You Shall Find

Isaac has a big problem. The sheep in his flock have gotten all mixed up! Can you help him count them?

How many sheep can you find?

©1992 Susan L. Lingo, Melissa C. Downey
Permission is granted to reproduce this page for classroom use only—not for resale.

Did you know that people's names mean different things? Back in the days of the Bible, when people chose names for their children they picked names that stood for their favorite foods, colors, or places or special words to describe their child.

When Sarah was 90 years old and Abraham was 100, God told them they would have a son. Sarah thought it was just a heavenly joke and laughed at the thought of having a baby at her age!

God knew how Sarah had laughed, but He always keeps His promises. Soon God blessed Sarah and Abraham with a tiny baby boy! God knew of the joy and laughter this baby would bring to Sarah and Abraham, so He told them to name the baby Isaac, which means laughter.

Today, many boys and girls are named after people in the Bible. Sometimes the names are shortened and are called nicknames. If your name is Joshua, you are probably called Josh. If your name is Andrew, perhaps you go by Andy. Some girls named Elizabeth shorten their names to Beth while others may call themselves Liz or Lisa. Although you may go by a shorter form of your name, your nickname means the same thing as your longer or "given" name.

Here are some common names in the Bible and what they mean:

Abraham—father of many   Peter—rock
Adam—man   Noah—comfort
Eve—living   Moses—draw out
Sarah—princess   Joshua—the Lord saves

Here are some names that are popular today and what each name means. See if *your* name is here!

Girls
Lindsay—peaceful one
Melissa—honeybee
Jane—God is gracious
Jennifer—fair

Boys
Ryan—little king
Charles—strong
Michael—from the Lord
Justin—upright

(Teacher: You may wish to bring in name books so students may look up their names and discover their meanings.)

"Give thanks to the Lord, call on His name" Psalm 105:1 (NIV).

©1992 Susan L. Lingo, Melissa C. Downey
Permission is granted to reproduce this page for classroom use only—not for resale.

Ancient Games

Children of Old Testament times played many of the same games you do. See if you know these games played by children long ago.

Knucklebones

Needed: pennies, beans, or small pebbles

Place one bean on the back of the hand. Toss it in the air and catch it with open palm up. On the next toss, use two beans. The next three, etc.

Arm Wrestling

Two players sit facing each other at either side of a table. Each rests his elbow on the table. Each player clasps the other's right hand (left hands may be used). On a signal, each tries to push the other's hand to the table. Elbows must be kept on the table.

Marbles 1-2-3

Needed: marbles (3 per player), masking tape

Using the masking tape, make 3, 5-inch circles, 4 to 5 feet apart on the floor. Also place a tape line 3 feet before the first "hole." Holes may be marked 1, 2, 3. The object of the game is for the player to shoot the marbles into the circles in the correct order. Each player may have 2 shots per hole. Scoring is optional but may be done by allowing 10 points per hole.

©1992 Susan L. Lingo, Melissa C. Downey
Permission is granted to reproduce this page for classroom use only—not for resale.

Fluffy Flock

Isaac had to help his father tend their flocks of sheep. Do you suppose that he ever tried to draw them in the sand?

Use a piece of paper and follow the leader!

Draw the sheep on half of a piece of paper. Glue two cotton balls on sheep. Fold the paper in half and stand your sheep up. Can you make a whole flock?

©1992 Susan L. Lingo, Melissa C. Downey
Permission is granted to reproduce this page for classroom use only—not for resale.

Family Fun

Are families really different today than long ago? Not so very much. Since the day God created our first mother and father, Adam and Eve, families have felt the Lord's love through our parents, brothers and sisters. And with God as our Abba Father and we His children, we all belong to the wonderfully loving and sharing family of God!

Share some family fun with the two ideas below.

Family Feelings Board
Hang a large piece of paper or posterboard on the refrigerator and put markers or crayons nearby. Family members draw or write little messages and pictures on the paper whenever they have a feeling to share. At the end of the day (or week), sit down and share your paper together!

Family Apple Trees
Have each person in your family put fingerprint apples on a tree you have colored. (Use red paint or a stamp pad for the apples.) Let each family member draw their face on their apple!

Did You Know?

If you had lived back in the time when Isaac was a child, you'd have called your father "Abba" instead of Dad. You would be living in tents with your grandparents, aunts, uncles, and lots of cousins to work and play with! Your family would be large, because life was not easy and all of the work would need to be shared. With no large grocery stores or department stores to shop for food and clothing, most of your family's days would be spent tending the family flocks of sheep, fixing meals, drawing water from the well, or making clothes from sheep hides.

Then, as today, families shared their work to keep households running smoothly.

©1992 Susan L. Lingo, Melissa C. Downey
Permission is granted to reproduce this page for classroom use only—not for resale.

Directions for making a family book:
1. Cut out book.
2. Fold on - - - line.
3. Draw pictures for each page.
4. Color your book.

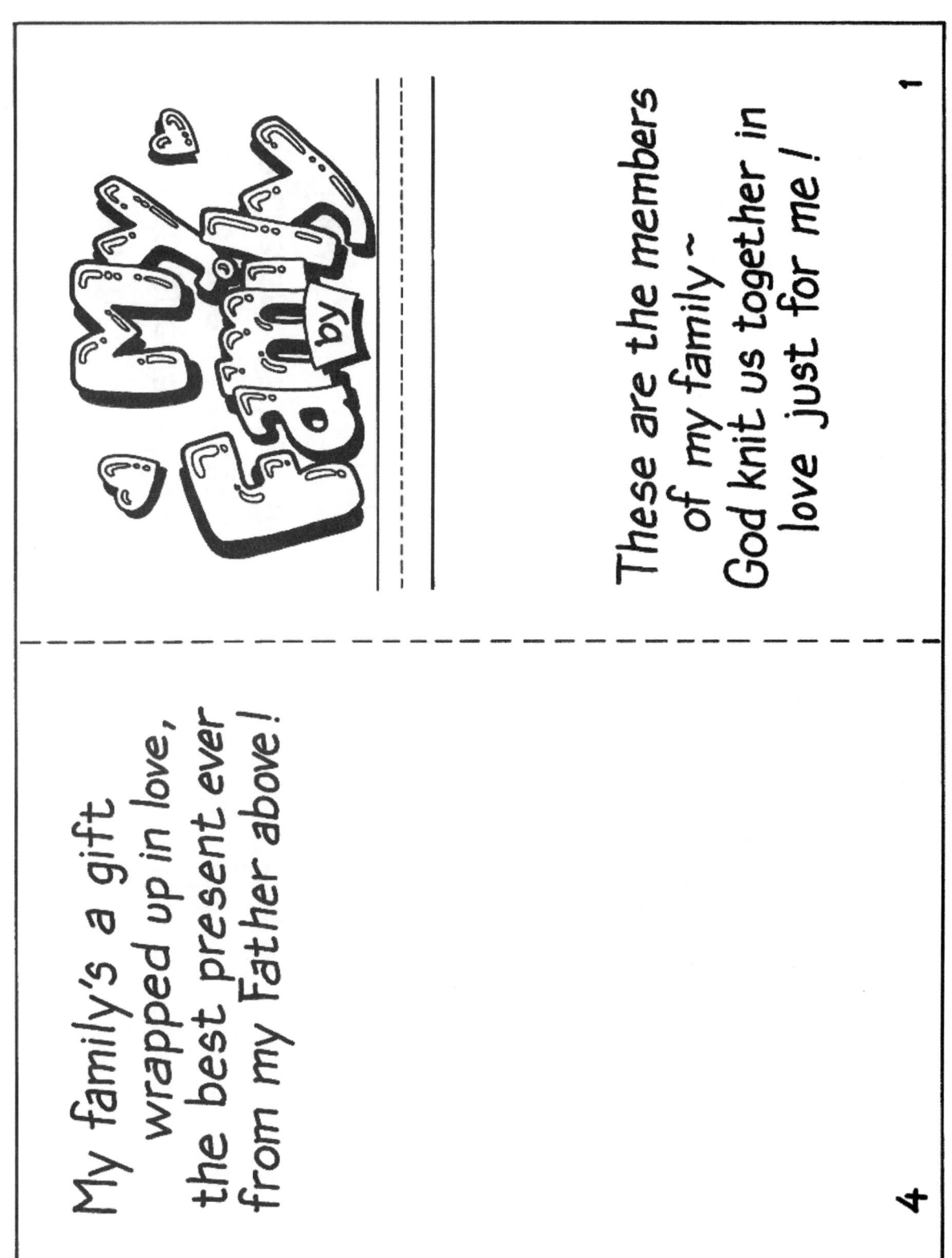

©1992 Susan L. Lingo, Melissa C. Downey
Permission is granted to reproduce this page for classroom use only—not for resale.

Sometimes we like to do special things; here's one of them... see the smiles that it brings?

Together we work and we laugh and we dream. We share it all 'cuz my family's a team!

©1992 Susan L. Lingo, Melissa C. Downey
Permission is granted to reproduce this page for classroom use only—not for resale.

Joyful Creations

To make this necklace, you will need:
string
wooden clothespin
black marker
cotton balls
glue
small pieces of paper

 Tie string in a loop to go easily over your head.

 Glue string to back of clothespin.

 Glue stretched out cotton balls over front and back of clothespin, except over face and bottom of "legs."

 With your marker, color legs and add a face.

 Tear out tiny ears from paper and color them black. Glue them on the sides of the head.

 Let your sheep dry for one day before you wear him!

"*I am the good shepherd; I know my sheep and my sheep know me...*"
John 10:14

©1992 Susan L. Lingo, Melissa C. Downey
Permission is granted to reproduce this page for classroom use only—not for resale.

Mountain Message

What did Abraham's heart tell him as he climbed the mountain with Isaac?

(Hint: Look at Proverbs 3:5, NIV.)

"

"

Abraham's Test

The poem below tells the story of Abraham's greatest act of faith and obedience. Read the poem and then complete the puzzle using Genesis 22:16, 17 (NIV) and the numbered words in the poem.

Isaac was a gentle one,
Sarah and Abraham's only(3) son.
An obedient child with eyes so bright,
He became Abraham's sole delight!

Then God came to Abraham
To test his belief,
saying, "Climb Mt. Moriah—
return Isaac to me!"

The(5) anguish and pain tore
Abraham apart,
But unfailing faith
was alive in(7) his heart!

The pain flowed so deep,
Yet far deeper still,
Was the faith and(1) the love
to trust in God's will.

He climbed Mt. Moriah
with unfailing trust;
His footsteps a-trudge
In a pathway of dust.

A shiny knife drawn
A tear in his eye,
"I'll love and obey You(2), my God,"
Was his cry.

And God heard his heart,
filled with love and with faith,
And(4) a ram was delivered
To take Isaac's place!

So Abraham learned
Through obedient giving,
Both faith and his son(6)
Were gloriously living!

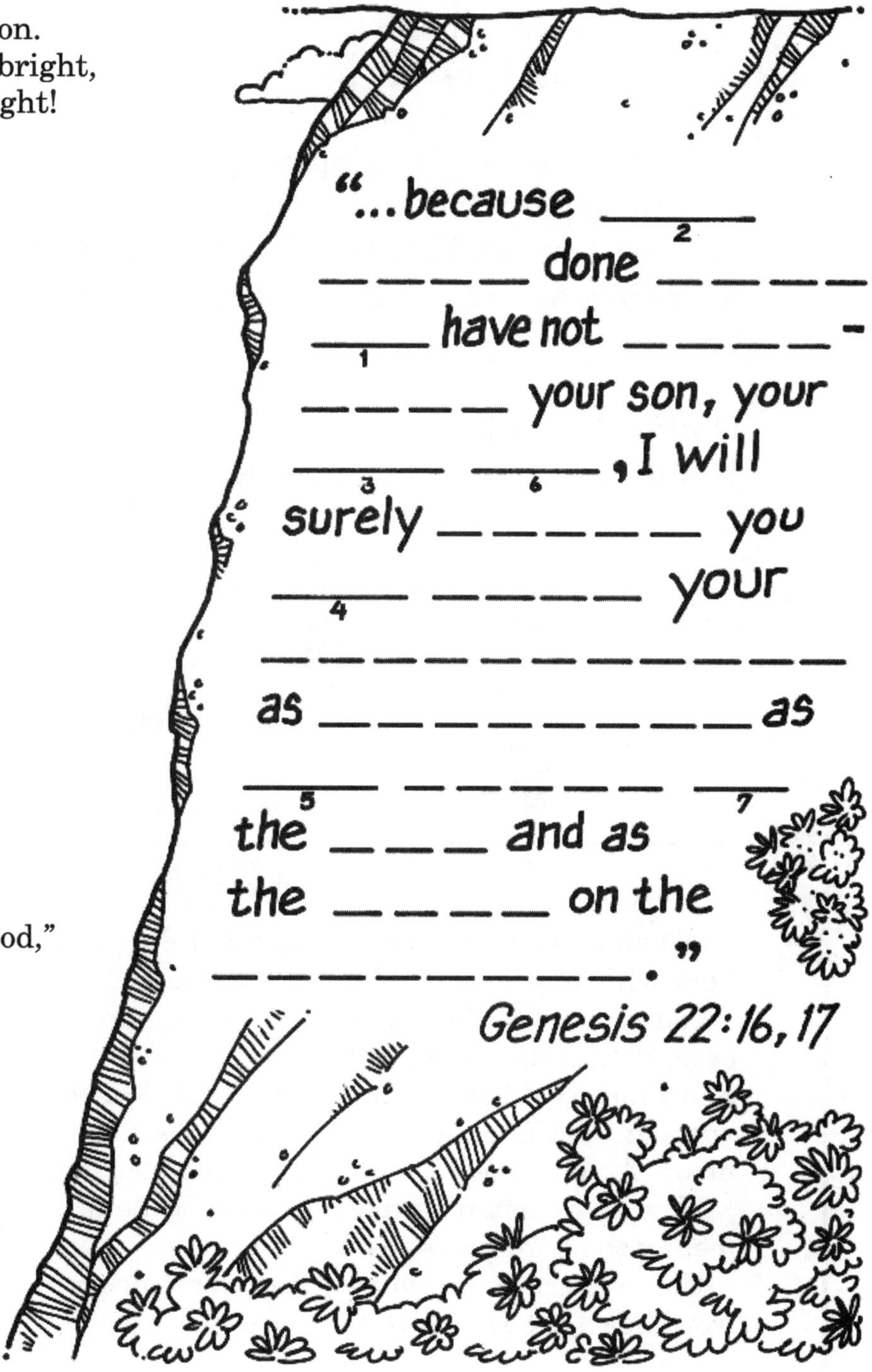

"...because _____ (2)
_____ done _____
___(1) have not _____ -
_____ your son, your
_____(3) _____(6) , I will
surely _____ you
_____(4) _____ your
_____ _____ _____
as _____ _____ as
_____ _____ _____
the _(5)_ and as _____(7)
the _____ on the
_____."

Genesis 22:16, 17

©1992 Susan L. Lingo, Melissa C. Downey
Permission is granted to reproduce this page for classroom use only—not for resale.

Kazoo

Needed: paper towel or toilet tissue roll
wax paper
rubber band
markers, art paper, tape—optional

1. Cut a 4 ½ to 5-inch square piece of wax paper.
2. Cut paper towel roll in half or use the the whole toilet tissue roll.
3. Cover one end of the roll with the square of wax paper.
4. Secure with the rubber band placed over the wax paper.
5. Decorate the kazoo.

Children may hum a favorite tune into the open end of the kazoo. Notice how the sound of the hum changes when using the kazoo!

Can a Heart Hear?

We all know that ears can hear, but did you know that you can also hear with your heart? When God spoke to Abraham, Abraham had to listen very carefully to the words of the Lord. Yes, he did listen with his ears, but he also listened with his heart! Abraham knew in his heart how much God loved him; how God filled his heart with love, faith, and wisdom. Abraham heard words with his ears. He heard love with his heart. And he knew he must trust and obey what God had spoken.

How do we listen with our hearts? By being very quiet, very still, and feeling the Lord's love inside.

Can a heart hear? Oh, yes! Just remember: the first four letters in the word heart are H-E-A-R!

"Be still, and know that I am God." Psalm 46:10 (NIV)

©1992 Susan L. Lingo, Melissa C. Downey
Permission is granted to reproduce this page for classroom use only—not for resale.

Merry Melodies

BOTTLE BAND

You need: eight bottles of the same size (GLASS) or any other GLASS containers of the same size; pencil or small dowel stick; water

Fill each of the eight containers with different amounts of water (for 12 oz. containers, fill one with 2 oz. of water, one with 3 oz., etc.). "Play" musical bottles by tapping with the pencil.

Variation

Instead of tapping the bottles, blow across the bottle tops to make hollow sounds. Can you "play" the song below? (Have some students play the song while others sing it.)

Listen With Your Heart
(Sung to the tune of "Jesus Loves Me")

Listen with your heart, dear one,
And you'll hear our Father's Son.
He will speak to you in love,
Sunshine words from God above!

Trust and obey Him,
Trust and obey Him,
Trust and obey Him,
He'll speak to you in love!

©1992 Susan L. Lingo, Melissa C. Downey
Permission is granted to reproduce this page for classroom use only—not for resale.

—SOUND EXPERIMENTS—

Mystery Sound Game

You need: a sack containing items that will make a distinct sound (examples: birthday horn, timer, beans in a can, paper to crumple) and slips of paper which describe sounds to make (examples: "snap your fingers," "imitate a bird call")

Have children sit in a circle. Select one child to draw a noise maker or slip of paper from the sack. Remaining children close their eyes while the person who is "it" makes the sound. The others will guess the sound. The first one to correctly guess the sound becomes "it."

Make Your Own Phone

Needed: 2 waxed paper cups;
        12 feet of string
        pointed scissors

Place a *tiny* hole in the bottom of each cup. Attach a cup to each end of the string by running the string through the hole from the outside bottom of the cup to the inside bottom of the cup. Tie a knot in the string to secure it in the cup. Stretch out the string until it is fairly tight—but not so tight that it pulls out of the cup. How loud do you need to talk to be heard? Can you hear a whisper?

Did You Know?

Sound is what comes from a very fast back-and-forth movement called *vibration*. Stretch a rubberband until it is tight and pluck it with your finger. Hear the twang? The sound vibrations travel through the air in tiny waves like ripples made by a pebble tossed into a pond. When the waves of sound enter the ear, they strike a tight piece of skin called the eardrum. The eardrum begins to vibrate and sends the sound waves all the way to the brain where it sorts out what has made the sound.

Sound and a Straw

Hum a constant sound into a straw by placing the end of the straw in your mouth, lips shut. As you hum, have someone begin to shorten the straw by cutting away the end. As the straw becomes shorter, the sound will go higher. Why? Because there is less room for the sound to vibrate, so the pitch (sound) goes higher. The more room (the longer the straw) the lower the pitch.

©1992 Susan L. Lingo, Melissa C. Downey
Permission is granted to reproduce this page for classroom use only—not for resale.

Trusted Path

Find the verse from Hebrews 11:11 (ICB) by traveling along the correct path. Pick up letters as you go and put them on the lines below.

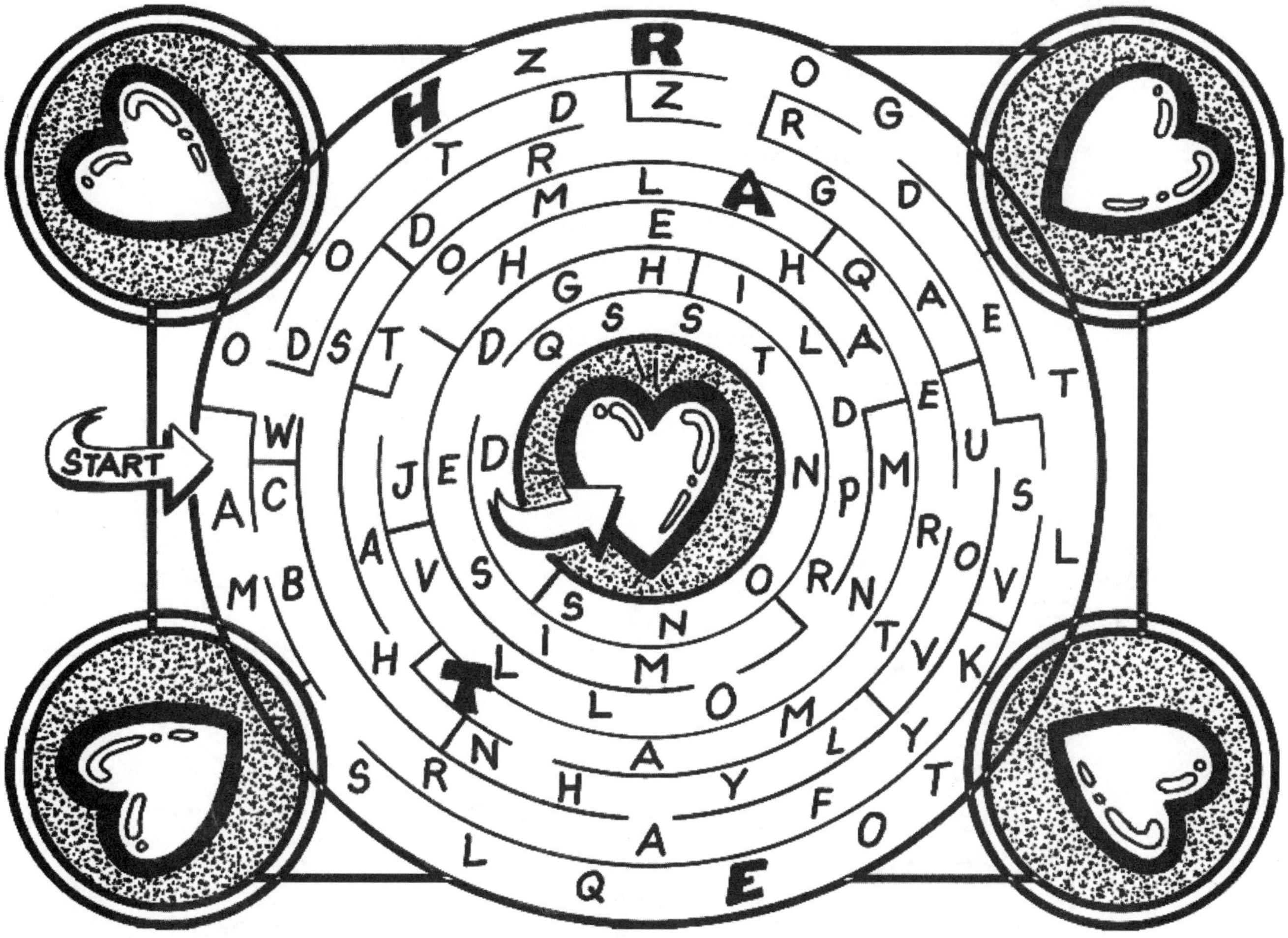

_____

_____

_____

Now unscramble the bold-faced letters to finish the sentence:

ABRAHAM TRUSTED GOD WITH HIS WHOLE _____!

©1992 Susan L. Lingo, Melissa C. Downey
Permission is granted to reproduce this page for classroom use only—not for resale.

How Small is a Whisper?

How small is a whisper? Just that small!
Sometimes it's barely there at all.

It tickles your ear like a summertime breeze;
It's dainty and sweet like a butterfly's sneeze!

As tiny and soft as a hummingbird sings,
Like air that is brushed by angels' wings.

How small is a whisper? Just that small!
Sometimes . . . it's barely there at all.

©1992 Susan L. Lingo, Melissa C. Downey
Permission is granted to reproduce this page for classroom use only—not for resale.

Trust Cookies

Ingredients:

½ cup melted butter or margarine
1 cup crushed graham crackers
1 cup flaked coconut
1 package (12 oz.) chocolate chips
1 cup chopped nuts
1 can sweetened condensed milk
1 pound of TRUST

Directions:

Layer ingredients, IN ORDER, in 9" x 12" pan.
DO NOT STIR! (Trust—remember?)
Bake at 325 degrees for 25 minutes or until brown.
Cool and cut into cookie bars.
ENJOY!

(makes 4 dozen)

©1992 Susan L. Lingo, Melissa C. Downey
Permission is granted to reproduce this page for classroom use only—not for resale.

Open any window; open any door.
God has given us glorious gifts
to seek, to find, to explore!

God's Gift Box

God's gift to Abraham was a listening heart.
Draw a picture of a gift God has given you.

©1992 Susan L. Lingo, Melissa C. Downey
Permission is granted to reproduce this page for classroom use only—not for resale.